Abigail Brown

by Heather Brett

Acknowledgements

Grateful acknowledgements are made to the following publications in which some of these poems first appeared: Cyphers, The Salmon, New Irish Writing, Krino, Stet, Raven Introductions 6, Iron.

A special thanks to Mary and Bernard Loughlin for the privilege of spending a year in Maggies Farm, Annaghmakerrig. Special thanks also to Philp Casey and Leland Bardwell for their encouragement over the years.

Cover by Heather Brett
Print Origination by Irish Typesetters, Galway
Printed by Colour Books Ltd, Dublin
Hardback binding by Kenny's Fine Binding

© Heather Brett 1991. All rights reserved

ISBN 0 948339 52 7 hardcover £8.50
ISBN 0 948339 53 5 softcover £4.95

Produced with the financial assistance of
The Arts Council/An Comhairle Ealaíon and
Galway Corporation.

Salmon Publishing
Bridge Mills, Galway.

for Kelly and Greg

Contents

Twin Elusives	1
The Burning	3
Under The Rhododendron	4
My First Real Winter	5
Tulips	7
Dream Time	8
Ringless	10
The Quality of Life	11
Vision	12
Things We Forget	13
Waiting	14
Glass Corridors	16
Blue Moon	17
Vegetarian, Shopping	19
Passing Time	20
Journey	21
One Indian Summer	22
For Tom	23
Walls	24
Abigail Brown	26
Elegy on a Saturday	27
Châtelaine	28
Searching for the Colosseum	29
Woolgathering	30
. . . And Afterwards	32
Sleeping Partners	33

The Coming	35
Shells and Empty Vessels	36
After Fire	37
Status Quo	38
Permutations	39
The Doppler Effect	40
Making Hay	41
The Unanswered Invitation	42
No Vacancies	44
Last Bus to Tallaght	46
Winter Distances	47
Old Shoes	48
Lesson	49
Love Song	50
Weeds	52

Twin Elusives

You have brought her in
by way of the yuppie garden
and through the maze of bonsai trees
have ignored
the raised stick branches
those monosyllabic whispers,
her glances, backwards.
You kept up a running commentary throughout,
showed her the spice plots
and the modest vineyard
prepared for next year's crop.

En route
your mother's roses stole the show!
Perfect Iceberg, Virgo, White Message,
wan blooms
like hard, starched Sunday underwear
too well trained
to allow that streak of errant colour
too scentless
to be objectionable.

At last, in the terraced cottage
you gave her a bed
and made her comfortable,
the kitchen walls of rough, basalt stone,

the sink concealed
behind a silk partition
and a titter of nervous laughter:
You played loud jazz
and Negro Spirituals
to drown out the silences.

At night
you placed her by a window.
In pale moonlight you undressed her
and held her so tightly
that no living thing
could breathe in the space between you.

But when you leave
a moon revolves
through an opened skylight
and in a ray of stardust
your lover quietly dances:
An Art Nouveau model for Winter,
a snow-bird, without sight of land.

The Burning

A white box
in a bottom drawer
holds folded red silk,

the creases like fire,
the lace just waiting to singe.
It smoulders beside letters,

old train ticket stubs,
last year's hotel receipts.
Some time in the night

a spark from her dream
will soar towards the silk
and ignite

and the morning,
like Joan of Arc,
will be charred.

Under The Rhododendron
for Urs

The drumlins round and
curve to a mute wait.

The two walking dip shoulders
jostling the light between.

That piece of blue, torn from the sky
floats bellydown on the lake

and a sudden shower fills the
fluted carmine cups,

drips from the lush green leaf.
I shelter

and turn to find you standing there
offering an umbrella

My First Real Winter

The postman says there'll be snow.
I take the proffered letter
and the bag, lost in the city
and posted back by my retired father,
his handwriting slanted and precise
on the label.
He said he'd visit when the weather got better.

The bag contains things I thought
I couldn't live without,
make-up, silk underwear, tapes
but I've managed without them
for ten whole colourless days.

The letter brings its own warmth,
words I can hardly decipher, written
in the freestyle of spontaneity and love,
without correction.

He talks about the holiday
we must have this coming summer:
everyone, it seems,
is concerned with the time of year.

I nestle under the duvet,
under the contents of the bag

and the pages of the letter.
Tomorrow I will rise and lag pipes,
seal window openings, split logs
and answer letters.
I have put off my first real winter
for a day.

Tulips

i. Tulips
of the garden
are shy things,
with tucked petals
prim and lean and subtle
retiring like dignitaries
among the green.

ii. Tulips
of the vase
grow greedy,
expand and ripen
blowzy and rude and loud
exposing their privates
like fat whores.

Dream Time

The field is high and wide
and thick with corngrass
and set apart
by a boundary of stout stone dykes,
crazy-paving up straight,
with round, three dimensional slates.

There are tractor tyre marks
by the gate
chevroned muck, dried hard by the sun
And an old tree to the left
with stones around the base
as if fallen, lying the way apples lie.

And I wear a dress of beige voile
with front brown lacing
and I'm sixteen again, following you.
(Please daddy, we didn't do anything,
we just walked and held hands
and kissed in a hayfield)

But you don't hear.
I spread a patterned rug
and my knees bend to make a double 'V'.
There's a white clover between my toes.

If you were with me now, the wind would flap
your shirt, your hand would be in your pocket.

I open dry white wine,
nibble on greengages and cheese
and think of your eyes, like black pearls
from some aborigine's Dream Time.
I settle and listen only
for the sound of you calling my name.

Ringless

She had a friend once who kept
pigeons; ringed and tagged and
charted,
some even, were given ridiculous names
like Yoyo
and Boomer
and were often monitored shitting:
Before she went
she shooed all the birds away,
let the cat in
and laid her ring in the loft.

The Quality of Life

My daughter sleeps beside me,
a little sun-browned squaw
with her hair plaited
and semi-circle of fringe.
I look at her
and hope she fares well in the world.
I lie awake and worry
missing the cigarettes I can't afford
wondering, where I go from here.
In the dark alone,
with no adult to reassure me
I dream up ways of conquering poverty
but dismiss them, one by one.
Maybe tomorrow I'll accost a stranger
drag him into the bushes
and set up my own beat
between here and Tallaght.
Maybe tomorrow I'll ring up Charlie Haughey
and tell him he needs me,
just send the mercedes,
or maybe not;
Each day dawns as hopeful and innocent
as the freckles across my daughters face.

Vision

I seem to be always following her,
that lithe, bright,
darkly dressed girl.
I can see her now,
skipping – yes – truly!
two hands on her hat brim,
her booted feet
dancing.
You'll say I'm fantasizing
 – making it up;
but I'm not,
she's real, out there somewhere,
and if I had
just another ounce of energy,
another spare rib
of confidence,
I'd be her!

Things We Forget

Funny how I can't remember you.
Strange to think
we shared a bed, a house,
children
in-laws, christenings and Christmasses.
Strange too, that I can't remember
how we touched, made love
or what we did together
for over a thousand days and a night.

But all that has gone
buried
by our weight
as we stomped on the grave,
hurtling away from each other
breathless
and dripping with spite.

When we meet now, we are wary,
sidestepping those paces between us.
Suspicious, like boxers after the fight.

Waiting

I close my eyes
   you are there
a pin-up on the inside of my eyelids:
I open my eyes
   you are there
a little distant, full-figure
I sleep
   you are there
ransacking my dreams,
I wake
   you are there
your absence filling my day.
I work
   you are there
intruding,
I relax,
   you are there,
taunting.
I eat
   you are there
scenting the food.
I drink
   you are there
elusive as fluid.
I smoke
   you are there

dissolving and forming at will.
I talk
   you are there
colouring my words,
I listen
   you are there
and it's always the leaving I hear.
I wait,
   not for you
but for the passing of all of this.

Glass Corridors

Now
I watch my daughter
and her friend
swop fancy paper,
eye their innocence in a body language
they have yet to master
and smile when she says:
'What was it like when you were a girl?'
There has been no divide,
no time
when I've been able to stand still
and with a certainty born
of fact or event, declare
I am not a girl anymore.
But for an instant she took me back
along glass corridors
hung with mottled mirrors,
the light falling through frameless windows
and I was a child again,
staring.
That look I've caught
on my mother's face
a thousand times.

Blue Moon

Once, every blue moon
it happens.
Despite the paranoia,
that old self-hate
that has my back in warbles
and reflects my face
as slightly par-boiled
and always over thirty.

The first time, I lied,
I was out to crucify
weighed down with gifts
I couldn't open
The old Russian doll act
– and inside was me
waving some pennant
with a message I couldn't read.

The second time, I knew better,
at least an apprentice
holder
of several tricks up my sleeve.
But what did I choose?
A yanker of hair,
biter of bare breasts,
rough handler of soft skin.

And this was number three.
I was ready
to let myself go
– but where?
when I turned again
there was no-one there
just a shuffling of lean shadows
in a wake of cooling air.

Vegetarian, Shopping

Doesn't all that rawness
make you ill?
I asked the butcher boy, blushing
behind the prime steaks
the wormy mince
the comma chops
the glistening liver,
stilled sheep's hearts,
the streaky rashers, resting trotters
and tied and bound pot roasts.
No, he said,
but God, I could murder a curry

Passing Time

And I will wait
and in my waiting I will
court every man
and boy
who lets me,
gathering seeds
and bitter herbs,
spices for the aftertaste
of a dish in my maturity
when I will sit and spit
and sift through
all the gobshite promises,
every passive bastard's dream
relish,
like the cat with the cream,
the only solitary solace left.
Like Lorelei,
I will wait

Journey

Up here, on this spiral stairway
there is stillness
and a muffled dark,
not so black that I could impose
but a muted dark,
soft with half-shapes of intrigue
and you can hear nothing
but how a bleak absence
might brush the inside of a conch.
I come alone here
stripped and without guile.
I know nothing
but wait for the cadence
to surround me.
I have never reached the last turn
always I hesitate
unsure of my right to go ahead.
But soon,
soon it will happen
and I will have no reasons left
for reluctance
and then I will fade,
somersault slowly into a thundercloud
and roll away

One Indian Summer
for Philip

September;
little breeze to fan the leaves
of trees
just enough
to dry the lines of clothes.
The kids could play without their coats
and shapes had shadows we'd forgotten;
A respite,
a last late harbour
for the migrating summer,
a wild tumble of golden-flecked colours
and the day as long as a winter's night.

For Tom

Is this the beginning then,
your end?
O Tom, to be really dead.
My friends seem to be dropping off slowly,
one by one
I suppose with the years
it'll gather speed
and towards the end
there will be a great rush of deaths,
the rest of us, waiting:
This reminds me of the cherry blossom
one snowflake of palest pink
and then a tinted storm like confetti.
But none of us were cherry blossoms,
you, more like some craggy bough
unsure, twisting and turning
from the trunk that sought you.
I don't know what I was then
happy to meet you at least
and glad to have you love me
for that short time.

Walls

These stone turrets
are cumbersome things,
and the way they dot
each separate landscape,
contradicts the fact,
that each is unique,
foundation sound
and formed to a singular, complex pattern.
Here and there
attempts have been made
to confuse the watchers,
the day-trippers
or lone hiker with his hunchback of necessities:
Then birds will ring around the Tower.
Spring flowers might sprout
from a sweet scented mulch,
caverns might appear inviting
but will always disappear
in a dead end.
When the light goes
human hands reach out
from hidden crevices,
stone cold fingers

finger familiar, worn outlines.
They reach to touch,
seek to recognise,
need to know.

Abigail Brown

There is sun today
summer sun
A real warmth
and the birds sing
I walk
and am drawn
not to living things
but to the cemetary:
'Abigail Brown, Killiney
died 13th June, 1881,
aged eighteen.
'My days are gone like a shadow
and I am withered like the grass.'

Elegy on a Saturday

I sit in a brightly lit kitchen,
half-listening to dogs barking
and Bob Seger working down his Night Moves.

It is quiet here and the kids are sleeping.
Each surface holds a book or a page
with a few words that meant something yesterday.

When I was young, I did my fair share of dating.
Now tables are turned, the years somehow upsetting
the balance, and I stay in more than I care to say.

Some days, I live to be a mother, gather my children
to me and give; We go and eat hamburgers and look
at toys in illuminated city store windows.

And somedays I'm just by myself, reading or writing
to unseen hosts of ones: Those days are silent
and transluscent,

perfect pockets, into which I drop
each gone minute, done day and every last
used second of being.

Châtelaine
for Anne

She half-lives
half-gives
half of herself
wondering, maybe,
what would've helped
but feels it's an issue
not worth the cause
– what's really gone
if you can't feel the loss?
She refuses to lower
to consider the blame,
thresholds she'll never
chance again
She's all opaque windows
sheltering pain,
a self-contained kitchen,
this Châtelaine.

Searching for the Colosseum

Another landmark
falls behind,
lost as I speed along this runway
and if I could attempt to plot this path
or even locate my present position
from some past point of recognition
to this blind spot,
I'd only end up lost.

Like when I try to piece this time together,
try to bundle up my life
into something solid,
something I could toss and catch
and toss again
like a smiling, swaddled infant,
I only fail
and there is nothing there for me
but pinned rags
strewn about the Liffey.

Woolgathering

I came from a family
that did not hug.
Touch was for smacking
and kisses for the dead,
the old dead.

I came from a family
that did not listen,
would not read between the lines,
and talk was for gossip
or ordering groceries.

I came from a family
that believed in face-values,
where priests and doctors and teachers
were right beyond question
and money was all or nothing.

I came from a family
of solid people,
Northern stock, roots planted in terra firma,
no heads in the clouds,
no tolerance for dreamers.

I see the end of that generation,
stout skeins of yarn, snapping and breaking,
feel the tug of a life made feeble
feel myself never so brittle,
spoilt for choice in a world of wanting, and

hearing only the simple word Home.

. . . And Afterwards

I knew that this could happen:
But as a shadow
slips inevitably ahead,
we did it anyway
– some silent elongations of ourselves entwined
and touched
and we followed.
O, I'm not saying that you weren't sweet,
nor that flesh and blood and bone
were lying,
but now it's different,
so very different.
Someone said he'd save a city
for one true man,
but in the end
we couldn't even save ourselves.
Now I'll have to change the colours
throughout this calling,
borrow a hairshirt vest from a friend of mine,
unpick the guilt and anger from this sculpture,
and sit a full dark week in the cellar.
O my love,
where is my black dress?

Sleeping Partners

I slept with an eagle
he was all talons
and cracked whispers
I had a long way to fall

I slept with a snake
but his scales were razors
and he never closed his eyes.
I had to use camouflage.

I slept with a red deer
he was all velvet and bone,
my wounds all under the skin,
O Sweet Jesus Pain

I slept with a shark
his teeth weren't the problem
but his eyes were death pebbles
and he kept staring

I slept with a rat,
he was fond of sharing me
my shame he distributed freely
I had no place to hide

Now, I sleep with spirits
my bed never so full,
phantoms play on the ceiling,
my bed is warm with skins.

The Coming

Some Christ has risen
endomorphic and white-robed
He moves among us.

In a far off hut
I lie between my lover's thighs
cheek against chest

misreading beat for tread.
I lie wide-eyed and waiting
knowing He will come.

In the city
already Its presence is felt.
Strong men topple off buildings

and young women are found
slain and rotting in alleys,
their faces covered

and their knees bare.
But my lover lies quietly
stroking my shoulder

while outside in the street
lintel paint blisters and peels
in the shape of a cross.

Shells and Empty Vessels

You shout
and I splinter
Not many like me, in half-a-dozen
you said, adding
Thank-God for good measure
along with the cold look,
the sneering smile.
Good.
I hope they break the mould that made me,
and send the chippings flying
to rain like pigeons' droppings
all about you.

After Fire

At the long moment of climax
I cried; sobs stole out of me
and I didn't know where the sadness
had come from, only that it
remained,
remained a long, long time.
And I knew I was beaten
felt the need in me seep away
weep through wounds you made
but never even noticed.
Only one of a hundred ways to die.

Status Quo

First and last
she's a mother
wife
housekeeper
maid
and absent father.
Inbetween, she has a lover
and is a mother
wife
housekeeper
maid
and absent father to him.
Someday,
she thinks,
Someday.

Permutations

Once,
I belonged to you,
more surely than
if you yourself
had opened some smooth contour
and given birth
and breathed into me your own sweet scent.
You cut the webbing between my fingers
pared away the dead flesh
painted colour in my cheeks,
lights in my eyes
and stopped my lips when I spoke of doubt.
You gave me purpose
I was your shadow
your happy will-o'-the wisp,
moth to your light
to your hot hot flame
that consumed me.
Now
I am a wise old bird
and I feast on human hearts
and make you watch
from the perch where I have trussed you
up by the heels
and when you sleep
I jab you, hard, with my cold,
bony, bloody beak.

The Doppler Effect

I've been looking for you
all my life,
since I first witnessed your birth
in the fragmented iris
of a lover so long ago
I recall only his taste.
You have that taste:
I was aware of you taking shape
from every man I bedded,
skins shed spores
and I watched you gather them up
for details later.
You have their scent.
I saw you once
on the otherside of a multitude;
You knew it was me
but you couldn't wait,
the tide was turning.
I know you now,
out there in the darkness
you hide behind each sapling,
blade of grass
or capital letter, waiting.
You have been looking for me
all my life.

Making Hay

Streaming sunlight wakens me,
throws the pattern of the net
across the ceiling
and stranded crescents
fatten like smiles
to march parallel along wall
and lampshade.
And I feel
there won't be many more of these.
Somehow,
us or the world,
one's going to end soon
and either will cut like coral.
But this morning
here in this room
filled with this shade of Wedgewood blue,
let's find some vacant limbo
some space
where our minds can wander
and our bodies talk.

The Unanswered Invitation

It's an old wind that blows tonight.
I can smell memories fraught with the scent
of dried grass
and they seek me out, no rest
no rest for the traveller
and bundled in my trenchcoat
I am bound for outside travel.

The invitation sits upon the mantelpiece
in full display
above a wide fire that never dies.
There are others dancing there,
old ghosts that swoon about the cleared room
all silk and finery and arched eyebrows.

But I can't go in.
I feel the road subside beneath my feet,
there's nothing solid anywhere and
the waves are ringing their arms like harpies.

But I edge around the tower,
hands clenching air like hope
searching for power that might still be
caught in pocket linings

I am a voyeur, naked under my coat
leaning well into the shadows
and it might be Christmas, and it might
be snowing
and I might be found in the morning
stiff and propped against windows,
French windows, that are only slightly open.

No Vacancies

There is only one chair by the fire,
my chair; the children play on the floor
or the sofa, soles upwards, and there is
a lack of family portraits.
There is no man in this scene.

This morning I opened the windows wide
to let your scent go, but all day
I could smell you, could feel your skin on mine
like a pressure, like the imprint of fingers
after the grasp is removed.

Tonight I sit in my chair, in my house.
The children draw and chat about the coming
communion. There is an audible silence when
they are quiet, and I wonder if it is I
who wedge open these small spaces – and for what?

I did not give you my chair last night.
There are boundaries everywhere that you cannot
cross, and I am quick to mention them,
too quick perhaps, to put you in your place,
too quick also, to assume mine.

But alone I look fondly on the things
I have here, the bits and pieces that we have

accumulated and collectively call mine.
The walls are missing nothing, the house
is furnished, we call it home.

All the rooms are taken, each bed spoken for.
Any cracks have long since been papered over
or filled in. We have no space left, no empty
drawers or anywhere where another might make himself
at home: There are no candles burning in the windows.

Last Bus to Tallaght

Stock still she stands,
his mouth
working on hers.
I watch
through my own reflection
and wonder,
and envy slightly,
her somebody,
that space filled between her arms,
the heed her lips receive,
the ceremony.

There have been times
when I've
wanted some body,
ached to find a wall of flesh
in the void
all strength and muscle and solidity.
Some body to covet,
to feel tendon and sinew and bone
and think of nothing

Winter Distances

She skates into the picture
without warning
swaning over slopes
packed tight as mexican firecrackers
and just to show she's mastered it
repeats figure-eights on the
underside of my skull.
The shavings of bone fly like snow.

This could go on forever,
for locked here
in this schizoid circle
I am bound to give her credence
and sometimes
she's so still, posing
with one knee bent, arms
a graceful arc – lethal.
On those days I too, go missing.
I also skate in Winter

Old Shoes

I take another's place now;
It's a hard task
to rid you of all the bad habits
and I admit
in places I've worn you through
to the bone,
but I'm not discouraged
even when you look at me and say
that when I've finished
you'll be all dressed up
with nowhere to go.
It could be true
but this law of substitutions
is an old trick:
Our tombstones will bear the work
of many, many hands.

Lesson

Once,
upon a time,
we met.

Autumn,
red stars on wet ground,
spill from coral sunsets

and walking
we startled two pheasants into flight,
the hen leading away

across a cellophane lake
to a perfect ring of pines,
ancient talisman

and I needed one
– the spell too brittle –
All perfect things have flaws.

And I remembered the pheasants.
I was the first to leave.

Love Song

Ours
is a seldom frequented skin.
It hangs alone
out there, waiting
where the unfulfilled come to water,
where a peach sun squats
and tints a sallow landscape
a spanish rosé.

I'll be your pear
in a flask of sweet wine
You be an orchard
on a summer hillside
and time
will just waste away.

And
on normal days
we'll dance the polyglide
with inherited patience,
left over symptoms
from some raw deal,
and we'll leave no shadow,
no imprint, no clue
as to who I am, as to who are you.

And I'll be your pear
in a flask of sweet wine,
You be my orchard
on a sunny hillside,
and time,
time will just waste away.

Weeds

In this garden, love, the weeds spring up
like chances,
numbering the days,
pinpointing this time of year
and I want to tell you
how my time here is going
how the scene from my window keeps changing,
how the transparent heather hides magenta
how the gorse, so hazy
can seem so alive.

Each morning I still walk these roads,
hands in pockets
wearing my usual black
– that absence of colour I'm fond of –
and I want to tell you
how the finest of chains can shorten
how the time gnawed,
how I've found the exact measure of a week here,
the singular minute
each rounded, separate pause.

Love, I couldn't sustain the intimacy
and I have no words to
soften the blow, nor
any way to dull their effect,

but I want to tell you
how this pattern for me keeps repeating,
how the search is never really over,
and the footsteps
though pointing forward
inevitably pull back.

Occasionally, I dream of failure
the fears
real, but transient things
and love, no matter how it goes
I want to tell you
that I could not barter for feelings
nor compromise this need,
nor do anything other
than accept
this metanoia, this destiny, these weeds.